Tether

tether

poems by Kirsten Dierking

Spout Press
Minneapolis, MN

Copyright © 2013 Kirsten Dierking

Kirsten Dierking
Tether
Poems

ISBN: 978-0-9835478-0-8

Cover Image: Jennifer Davis
Book Design: Chris Watercott
Cover Design: John Colburn
Interior Artwork: Kimber Olson

First Edition
Printed in the United States of America

Spout Press is a member of CLMP and is distributed
to the trade by Small Press Distribution, Berkeley, CA
(www.spdbooks.org)

Published by Spout Press
PO Box 581067
Minneapolis, MN 55458-1067
www.spoutpress.org

ACKNOWLEDGEMENTS

I am indebted to the McKnight Foundation for a generous Artist Fellowship that allowed me to complete this book, and to the Banfill-Locke Center for the Arts for a writing residency funded by a Medtronic Arts Access Grant through COMPAS. I am also grateful for past financial support from the Minnesota State Arts Board, the Loft Literary Center, SASE: The Write Place, and the Jerome Foundation.

I am grateful to Garrison Keillor and everyone at *The Writer's Almanac* for their support of poetry, and for reading my poems on the radio.

More than mere thanks to my family, friends, and mentors who helped with this book in so many ways — from editing and revising, to support and encouragement, to inspiring conversation: Patrick Dierking, Michelle Filkins, Floyd Paurus, Nancy Paurus, Robin Paurus, Leslie Rentmeester, Dianne Gray, Kay Korsgaard, Teresa Boyer, Carol Pearce Bjorlie, Ann Iverson, Janet Jerve, Marie Rickmyer, Kathy Weihe, Liz Weir, Tracy Youngblom Turner, Lia Rivamonte, Kimber Olson, Tim Nolan, Todd Boss, Sharon Chmielarz, Ann Schroder, Talia Nadir, Imani Jaafar-Mohammad, John Colburn, Beth Virtanen, Susan Carol Hauser, Roseann Lloyd, Deborah Keenan, Mary Rockcastle, Mary Ellen Flannery and my fellow *Thought & Action* panelists, Bob Jones and all the Minnesota USATF throwers, my colleagues, students, and the Philosophy/Humanities Department at Anoka-Ramsey Community College, everyone concerned with the writing program at Hamline University, the writers and artists at Banfill-Locke — and so many others.

CREDITS

Many thanks to the following publications, where these poems previously appeared (some with different titles):

- *The Comstock Review*: "Kayak"
- *The Emprise Review*: "In February, Think of Mexico" "Eclipse" "The Last Cold Thing" "The Forest" & "Mississippi"
- *The Finnish North American Literature Association Newsletter*: "In Early Evening"
- *Green Blade*: "Lilacs" "Wilderness" "Daedalus and Icarus - A Painting by Riminaldi"
- *Imagination and Place*: "Thunder"
- *The Minneapolis Star Tribune*: "Body of Water"
- *Off Channel*: "The August Launch of Discovery" "Humanities"
- *The Taste of Permanence*: "After Labor Day"
- *What Light Poetry Project, MNArtists.org*: "Half Asleep"

CONTENTS

THE EBB TIDE

Half Asleep	5
Thunder	7
The Gray Cat	11
Eclipse	12
For a Year I Write Poems in an Inn Built in 1847 in a Room That People Say is Haunted by a Ghost Named Nathaniel	14
Darkness, Distance, Nightfall	15

THE VISIBLE CURRENT

Tilt	23
Deep Winter	24
In February, Think of Mexico	26
Peacock	27
The Last Cold Thing	28
Release	29
Kayak	30
Wilderness	32
The August Launch of *Discovery*	33
After Labor Day	35
Mississippi	36

BODY OF WATER

Lilacs	43
Daedalus and Icarus—A Painting by Riminaldi	44
Slope	45
Soup	46
The Forest	48
Coyotes	49
Nightfall on Superior	51
Becalmed	52
After You Left for Your Mother's Funeral	53
Body of Water	54
Something Else	55
Greenwich	56
Time Travel	57

THE BALM OF THE SEA

How to Stop Time in the Seam Between Two Dangerous Places	63
Nuthatch	65
Unresolved	66
Humanities	67
What I Won't Know	68
Tether	69
The Eight-Below Earth	70
In Early Evening	72

For Patrick, Floyd, Nancy, Robin, Leslie

THE EBB TIDE

"I slept as I have not slept for—for Heaven knows how long, my body lying peacefully at last…"

"There is nothing to be done without sleep," said Stephen.

—Patrick O'Brian, *The Wine-Dark Sea*

HALF ASLEEP

Someone is walking with you in their arms
the way you haven't been carried, swaying,

since you were a child. No whispers, not a wisp
of where it is you might be going, it could be

your spouse stepping over the fairy-tale
of your new marriage, it might be a fireman

lifting you out of your burning house.
The bones of your neck arch beautifully

backward, throat open to anyone's judgment,
as you wane into the warm shoulder

of this great undemanding etherealness,
as if the way you really are could be easily

embraced and hardly a burden to anyone.

THUNDER

I.

In the first spring storm of the season,
my husband says *we forget half our life has thunder.*

II.

It is mostly the sound of distant misses
and missed misfortunes. The whole world

doing dangerous things, while we lay together
as if we were the world's first animal pack,

and feeling, just by virtue of our limbs touching
and just by being not alone, undamageable,

and the most hopeful sense of protection.

III.

We were in bed when lightning hit the house next door,
a vicious fire quickly licking through the roof,

how trained we were from television to repeat the proper
platitudes to the uninjured but newly homeless.

Later that day, our tongues still thick with the taste
of ash and watered smoke, our talk hummed with a hint

of excitement, even triumph, that we had been so close
to danger and the strike had fallen somewhere else.

IV.

She looked through the picture window
of her new house, this house standing

precisely where the first one had stood,
and the window looks on the same scene—

empty park, lake filling with August weeds,
and she said *the view looks unfamiliar*

when you know the world can erupt in fire
at any time, at any given explosive moment.

V.

An old oak lies between two living trees,
no trace of the long ago lightning strike

that split the trunk, just this tender,
softening wood, and sheltered inside

maybe a small animal or two. I think
I would like to lie like that, spent body
waiting for cover and all the love
of the coming snow.

VI.

I open the window to a storm coming,
the thick electric humidity, the static

standing-on-end of leaves, the trees
and grass rapacious for reaching

ever upwards, ever anxious to further
entwine their roots and greens, ardent

always for more moisture to make
more and more of themselves,

and it comes now, not gently,
but with all the deluge of passion.

VII.

In the basement, under the stairs,
curled around the quivering dog,

clothes wet with the sweat of knowing
life sometimes depends on luck,

the howling wind drowns the shake
of the rattling house and masks

the crack of two great pines as they
crash in the yard, just a few feet away.

VIII.

There are few worse sounds in summer
than the searing wail of tornado sirens.

Yet look how easily we forget
what drives us into the basement

as soon as the season begins to change.
Memory is sometimes kind, and given time,

you often can put losses behind you.
And yet, this same forgetfulness

must be what keeps us starting wars,
each generation the fresh launch

of a raw season, as if we had not
cowered in shelters, as if it had not

thundered before.

IX.

Hobbes said humanity is always prone
to fighting wars, but if prevented

all other time is peace.

X.

If only half our life has thunder,
think of all the peaceable parts.

The hush of snow in the early
morning as you twine your fingers

through white sheets and into
the open hand of your partner

and remember you have hours before
there is anywhere or anyone else

you need to be. *All other time is peace.*
The clouds hold together seamlessly.

THE GRAY CAT

Sometimes I stay awake as late as I can
so when at last I lie down, I fall asleep
without thinking for even a minute.

Sometimes I close my eyes and drift,
imagine myself in a little boat
floating under the swallows' nests
snug under the beams of bridges.

Sometimes consciousness slips away
the same way I set down the gray cat—
her quicksilver body sluicing like water
through the channel of my letting go hands.

ECLIPSE

I.

Red light fills the space between the pages of day and night,
a sailor's sign that tomorrow's passage will be untroubled.
The sun takes its scorch and fire somewhere else, while we sink,
if not into the respite of night, at least into hours of cooling.

II.

In a dark room at 4 a.m., vision means coming to see
after long adjustment. Even then, it means shadows.
The time you thought you were running out of all day long
has pooled here, a deep well of endless minutes with little current.
You know there are others who lie with their eyes wide open
in various beds across the country. You picture a string of
irregular pearls, small irritations in the soft shell body of sleep.

III.

The dog lying under your hand was once a wolf
who understands the hard-earned peace of a friendly
darkness. Like a tug tied to a tossing boat, she leans
against you, nudges you into the ebbing tide. Trust her
as she sighs herself into the pleasant tonic of sleep—
tonight it's going to be safe to dream.

IV.

You are on a great ship surging around the harbinger
of good and bad weather. When you wake again,
adrift on the intractable waves of consciousness,
you're grateful for the clement sun, the way it seems
to hang so eastward that all you've planned feels possible,
that this day will abound in light.

FOR A YEAR I WRITE POEMS IN AN INN BUILT IN 1847 IN A ROOM THAT PEOPLE SAY IS HAUNTED BY A GHOST NAMED NATHANIEL

The ghost stands
next to the window,
content inside
a preserved bubble
of summer day
that rises from
the grounds
and foundation.

When he first arrived
(in real life he means)
he tumbled into his
first real bed in weeks—
thought he had died
and gone to heaven.

Now, the days
are always warm
but flickering—
it is, he says,
like living inside
a candle flame.

DARKNESS, DISTANCE, NIGHTFALL

Darkness:

Coming home to the comforting shadows
of your own bedroom, to the clean sheets
of a sanctuary where all the voices at night
are friends—rain on the skylight, wind through
the maple, thunder somewhere far to the north.

But sometimes things can creep inside the seams
of darkness—the criminal who tests the locks,
the nightmare you imagined yourself, the pain
that makes you the only one sleepless inside
the extinguished house.

Distance:

The beauty of vastness—the surge of the ocean
as it rolls over the edge of horizon, the gentle arc
where it lays along the skin of the earth. The long
distance you've built between your former self
and who you've worked so hard to become.
How far away you feel from trouble as you
break a trail through the snow in the woods.

The distance that makes you forget the things
he most liked to eat for dinner. The fear of finally
going too far—finding yourself lost in a forest,
caught in a riptide, speaking the wrong,
unretractable words. The effort it takes to look

for beauty in emptiness—the prairie in winter,
the wind skimming the hard waves of drifted snow.

Nightfall:

The softness of the gray pause between
the sunset and early night. The winding down
of the day's work, the finishing of the dinner dishes,
the low drone of voices calling a baseball game,
the resting without yet needing to close your eyes.

Sometimes, the fearfulness of one more day
already gone. The shameful thought
that you'd really like to live forever,
even if it means loneliness.

THE VISIBLE CURRENT

It was not until sunset that the weather began to have a direction and some sort of a meaning.

—Patrick O'Brian, *The Far Side of the World*

TILT

I.

The bird feeder holds only the haze of the changing season.
Public places close early, slow-falling drafts
of diminishing light sift through vacant atriums.
Was I meant to be this gray, only two days into November?

II.

Winter this year is not a success. No one walks the streets
except the plushly coated Great Pyrenees Mountain dog.
The branches of the evergreens maintain their color, but have
to grow needles to do so. How could any profound thought
evolve in this dearth of daylight hours? The heat hums
through dusty ducts, the afternoons are downhills diving
toward early bedtimes, even the mouse in her dirty, linty,
basement nest sleeps as the traps are set in place.

III.

Into the greening grass we shuffle, our toes stained
with the smudge of mulch everything is erupting out of,
relieved to feel as beautiful as we'd ever been in early spring,
the threat of clippers and whirring mowers can't stop
our urgent growing, our breeding thickly, and what little
regret we feel for the loss of the old, wrinkled bark as it
gives way to a moist, unblemished adornment of leaves.

IV.

Summer bursts into humid profusion one June day
as if the stoic drone of insects had always hummed
across your eardrums. Patience blooms as the evenings
extend and once again there seems to be sufficient time
to become who you really wanted to be. Conveniently,
what you want right now is precisely this, nothing more
than the greatest distance the earth may tilt away
from the cold, nothing more than the sky replete with heat
and blue right until the very moment you must grow tired,
the mouse holds still, and the owl turns her head in the twilight.

DEEP WINTER

Make the cold
a blanket that mutes

the demands of the world
a drape to diffuse

the distance between
your grasping hand

and all you think
you're reaching for.

Think of these days
as a trail of reindeer

crossing the tundra,
antlers branched

in sprays of bone
against the sky.

Don't ask where
they are heading.

Don't ask the ache
of snow to stop falling.

IN FEBRUARY, THINK OF MEXICO

Leave behind
the cold thoughts
you can't carry.

Move south
until you are
an orchid
or a pink hibiscus.

Be a bird
with indigo wings,
a lemon yellow
angelfish.

Be the surf
and then become
the rising tide
and set your burdens
down on shore:

the coral bones
and bits of shell
and husks of all
the bygone things.

Be the blue
sigh of the ocean
gently pulled
from land
by the moon.

PEACOCK

In the middle of winter I stand
by the window, caught by the
cloudy pearl of the sky.

Don't close the window blinds
to keep the warmth—let the heat
go out, let the beauty pour in.

***

Asleep on a patio on a tropical island,
surrounded by palms and flower gardens,
I snap awake and lift my head and meet
the eyes of a startled peacock—
the gleam of his feathered sapphire breast,
trembling fringe of sea-colored crest,
his deep, indignant intake of breath,
iridescent bit of god,

and then he's gone, before I can speak,
before I try to give him a name.

***

Wouldn't it be nice if this is how
it could be at dying—
let the warmth go slowly out,
all the while some unexpected
sublime beauty pours in?

THE LAST COLD THING

If that visible current under the ice was the germ
of heat. If that small mound of dirty snow

was the last cold thing. If it was the end of a season
you had come to resent, yet the only winter of a year

you were never getting again, then it was, as always,
the story of life, even your own contrary life, and how,

just as the sun is warming you might go back to the frost again
if it meant growing a little younger. If only there was

a simple way to spring forward and change the clocks,
as if those hands sweeping through a lost hour

were nothing more than a household task—not a symbol
or metaphor, not some terrible presentment, if only

we had, every so often, a brief respite—a day filled
with plain-spoken words, a night without a secretive dream,

maybe even a boon or misfortune we might simply accept
as random and never wrestle to understand. In early spring

I watch two kids with fishing poles walk down to the river.
I let them go without thinking about their hunger, about

the hook, about how it feels to the fish.

RELEASE

In early May, I watch a boy fish the creek;
a short cast, then he spins the reel,
a smallmouth bass at the end of the pole.

It's the first nice day after the grind
of a hard winter, and I'm surprised
that mere pleasantness—the trees
just beginning to leaf, the waterbirds
splashing about—should feel so crucial,
a sweet and heavy flush in the heart,

the way the water feels to the fish
when the boy removes the ragged hook
and places the bass back in the shallows.

KAYAK

Minnows flash
sudden shafts

of silver light,
frogs stutter

guttural vowels
along the shore,

you feel like life
will go on and on,

if not this heron's,
if not your own,

then all the essence
of everything

that gives this lake
its wilderness—

all the bones
that rustle along

the shore today,
all the fuel

for future flesh
for new fish,

perch, birch,
the ever blooming

water flowers,
and you, for once,

moving without
difficulty

between the blues
of water and sky,

why not
rest your mouth,

let the words
in which

you think too much
spill out

and drift
to the bottom.

WILDERNESS

The first few days we have
slow mornings out on the lake,
long afternoons to walk in the woods,
evenings of leisurely innings of baseball
unwinding over the radio.

But time moves faster as the days
of the week accumulate behind us.
Friday passes in a flash of ease,
only now and again it seems the waves
washing on shore have reached an ending.

At dinner I say, tomorrow morning
it's back to real life, you sweep your hand
through the last of the day and say
there's nothing unreal about this.

But the scent of pine is faint on my skin,
as if I had been a wilderness once,
as we merge into traffic, as the lake
falls farther away behind us.

THE AUGUST LAUNCH OF *DISCOVERY*

By the time the creek
reaches this bridge

it's almost the Mississippi,
ready to slip

through the swale
of the country,

down to the whales
in the wide ocean,

the flickering salty
underworlds,

while just last night
seven people

passed across
the stratosphere

to sail the starry
edges of space.

Freud believed
happiness has

diminishing returns,
and so, I suppose,

we leave the things
that used to please us

so much more
than they please us now.

After awhile I walk away
from the sunlit bridge,

the water quits the creek
for the river

and only the astronauts
peering at earth

from a dark distance
are more in love

with all the things
they've left behind.

AFTER LABOR DAY

I can feel it now, the end of heat
rising from pavement, the last
of the close-fitting humid air.
As we drive by the airport,
an endless line of planes
turns south, their gray contrails
hazy over the green oaks,
the sultry breath of the lush world
shallower now.

I try to learn the humility
to bend to the seasons, the way
the oaks so unprotestingly
bow their heads in the wake of jets.
The way I imagine nothing more
than a sharp gasp at the first
crispness, oncoming russet,
before a sigh into relaxation,
the purity of no more choices,
the nowhere left to go but sleep.

MISSISSIPPI

The water flows with quiet persistence
toward some kind of finishing point

maybe as far as the glamour of a distant
sea, maybe only as far as the muck and

blowsy cattails hidden behind the next bend.
It's late September, and the first cold gust

has just come shivering down the river,
brushing across your bare arms with a touch

that feels both commonplace and ominous,
like passing your hand through a spider's web.

You think about sinking your fist into the
current and releasing what you long to keep—

this bright sun on open water, or even just
this quiet hour—and letting it pass away

from you, as easy as that. What is it like
to float without any resistance anywhere

the world wants? You slip into the sandy
shallows, plant your feet here, then here.

But the current only detours a moment
around your ankles, that flesh and bone

you're so very fond of, and flows on.

BODY OF WATER

The ship was tearing through the sea…But this was no longer the exhilarating pace of a few hours ago; now there was a nightmare, breakneck quality about it…

—Patrick O'Brian, *Desolation Island*

LILACS

On the day of my birth,
I bury my face in purple flowers
and breathe a scent so familiar,

I can't remember a childhood house
with lilac bushes, maybe it was
my mother who held the baby up

to the dense blossoms, maybe it was
my first pleasure, my mother whispering
breathe deep, it goes so fast.

DAEDALUS AND ICARUS—
A PAINTING BY RIMINALDI

Daedalus is so intent
on strapping the wings to Icarus,
he doesn't notice his beautiful son
radiating the nerve of the young,
the well-muscled,

but there it is—
in the cock of the head,
the unsubmissive flight of the eyes,
the lids too casually sliding down—
did he never show that face to his father?

Daedalus muttering stay close,
fly low to the ground,
but this isn't a boy
you can trust with wings.

Look at his pleasure as he
raises his hand up to the light.
Restless for stars, ready to clasp
everything bright.

SLOPE

If you have seen the snowcaps cling to the mountain tops
even in summer, then you know the earthbound rules

don't always apply and some cold things defy even
persistent warmth. If you want an untrammeled

moment of beauty, you need a conscious act of forgetting,
a moment of seeing only the angular sunlit rock, only

a flourish of graphite ridge, of not remembering
who you're missing and all you've missed, and not even

telling yourself this is the balm the world gives to ease
each little unhappiness. If you have tried to slow the future

by standing next to immovable mountains, you understand
those ponderous shadows will claim even a steadfast body,

and yet the dusk won't feel like granite, or even something
terribly hard, but more like the dark of a lake at night,

something you could slip easily under.

SOUP

Today in my
fortune cookie:

*Serious trouble
will bypass you.*

Does this mean
the cellphone will

run out of minutes,
the dog will be

sick on the rug,
but unemployment

and cruel disease
will sail on by

like hawks with
already full bellies?

And if the raptors
pass me by,

how far away
will they perch?

On someone I love?
On the stranger

at the next table,
feathers falling

into her hot
and sour soup?

THE FOREST

Two deer crash down the slope and hurtle into
the wiry stems of undergrowth, disappear
into what to them looks like more and more

of the same, thickets of chokecherry, sumac
and fir, entangled branches of aspen and oak.
As far as they know, these woods

are a never-ending expanse, when really
we're inside a park, a remnant of forest,
surrounded by houses, sidewalks and roads.

So many invisible borders—the moon
slipping from full to wane, the last shadow
cast before dark. The deer believe

they've entered a forest and every morning
most of us enter our days expecting
they'll sprawl ahead for a while,

that this day will not be the day the trees thin
and we find we're at the edge of a road,
our fragile animal hearts pounding.

COYOTES

At best, she only seems to nap, put to bed so openly.

At best, the line between wake and sleep is terribly thin,
both for the drugged and for those who sit close to their
sides, numbed by the flow of numbers across the
computer screen: heartbeat, oxygen, pressure, breath.

You learn to punch the button to spring the doors apart
to the ICU, learn to feed her, how to tug the sheet
to move her. She says time doesn't seem to pass.
When you look out the window, it's always the same—
a gray faded February hour.

You can't understand how anyone is able to work here
in the midst of people tethered to so many machines.

At the cash register, they tell you to have
an *awesome* day every time you buy your tea,
or lunch, or dinner. On the loudspeaker,
they play a little lullaby every time a baby is born.

One day, you pass a new father coming through
the hospital doors, clutching a new baby carrier,
the look on his face—scared shitless.

The nurses you feel intimately tied to
finish their shifts and go home.

Such a maelstrom of animal bodies, functioning,
dysfunctioning. Even a collie and black lab
square their shoulders, dogged in their therapy work.

On the walking trail in the field at the end of the parking lot
is a sign that says "this is a known coyote area—
if you are confronted—don't run—if you are afraid—
carry a stick." You walk with your empty hands
in your pockets, all bravado.

NIGHTFALL ON SUPERIOR

Is not night and more night coming on?
—Nietzsche

Standing on a high cliff above the lake,
water spreading to the dark border
of evening sky, it's easy to sense
the globe's roll, as if you're hanging
just at the top of a ferris wheel,
that pause before the gravity-less
downward lurch into space.

It's not the darkness that overtakes us,
but our own bodies carried forward
to lightlessness, even as we're
standing still, even as we step back
from the loose rock on the cliff's edge,
from the birch with all her exposed roots
incrementally slipping over.

BECALMED

Tonight I dream
of finding myself

in a small boat
becalmed on a sea

of pearly water.
Nothing to think of

on any horizon,
the constant flux

of forward motion
gently stopped.

AFTER YOU LEFT FOR YOUR MOTHER'S FUNERAL

My hands sort
through an old box
where I find a ring
you bought me at
a convenience store
twenty-five years ago
on our second date.

I think of your hands
fifteen hundred
miles away
gently folding up
her clothes.

I wish I was there.
We would hold hands
as we always do,
abiding.

BODY OF WATER
after the 35W bridge collapsed into the Mississippi River, killing thirteen

A white egret
flies across

the blue channel
with a fluid,

rhythmic
sweep of wings,

it's something
much less

than comfort—
a mere

feather-weight
of easing—

to see
one creature

lovely
and unassailable,

passing easily
over water.

SOMETHING ELSE

How good to be something else for awhile.

If you can't be water, sit amid the fragrant salts

of a blue bath.

If you can't be thunder, cry under a clouded sky.

Press your hands to the stone of your breastbone.

Enter the swift of the sweet downriver.

Be the rock the river refines.

The sleep in the slanting afternoon sun.

The brown bird perched in her invisible berth

in a brown tree.

GREENWICH

At the naval museum I look at Nelson's uniform, the one
he was wearing the day he was killed, and the bullet's damage
to the blue coat is surprisingly slight.

Just before he died he said *thank God I have done my duty.*
He must have been a little afraid of not being able to do
the heroic work required of him.

It's a lovely day in late March, the sun and daffodils are out.
We walk to the observatory, straddle the prime meridian,
try to feel our blood flowing back and forth between hemispheres.

There's a lot of laughter, young people clowning around,
adults striking silly poses for photographs. And why not?
One day, won't we all have to be brave?

TIME TRAVEL

I would begin at dawn
on July twenty-seventh,
when our dog suddenly
couldn't stand

and move back
until it was the first day
we lived together
in this new house,

the clocks
still packed in boxes,
the hours not yet
affixed to the walls.

THE BALM OF THE SEA

"You do not mean there is danger of peace?" cried Jack

—Patrick O'Brian, *Desolation Island*

HOW TO STOP TIME IN THE SEAM BETWEEN TWO DANGEROUS PLACES

Walk across
the wide beach
of white sand.
The bleached grains
of coral bone
will knead the soles
of your bare feet.

Enter the balm
of the turquoise sea.

Wade with care
through a silver ribbon
of black-eyed fish,
their supple school
will part to stream
around your hips.

Sink down
and draw the brine
over your lips.

Spread your body
across the seam
of shallow water,
your eyes skyward,
your arms cast out

let go
of all you grip
close to your heart.

Rise and slide
through crest and trough.

The waves will push you
neither in or out.

NUTHATCH

What if a sleek, grey-feathered nuthatch
flew from a tree and offered to perch
on your left shoulder, accompany you

on all your journeys? Nowhere fancy,
just the brief everyday walks, from garage
to house, from house to mailbox, from
the store to your car in the parking lot.

The slight pressure of small claws
clasping your skin, a flutter of wings
every so often at the edge of vision.

And what if he never asked you to be
anything? Wouldn't that be so much
nicer than being alone? So much easier
than trying to think of something to say?

UNRESOLVED

A man stood at the edge of the road with his hand out and a sign
that said "absolute desperation" and I didn't give him any money.

The obituary that mentioned the book
a woman was reading when she passed away.

The things I imagine, over and over,
I might have done to save Brian.

The dirty clothes on the laundry room floor I can't wash
because they smell of the salted ocean.

The mail in my inbox I don't answer, but don't delete.

What the painter David said about the three hundred people
he condemned to death in the Reign of Terror:

*"I thought an upright heart would suffice, but I was lacking
in the second quality, by which I mean, insight."*

HUMANITIES

There is something practiced, even choreographed
about measuring out a distance from things

that hurt too much. Today we covered Equiano,
the middle passage, the slave trade. Afterwards,

I could see in their faces, they had not yet learned
to slip smoothly past their terrible emotions

as if they were acquaintances they need not stop
to greet that day. Increasingly, I find myself

relieved to return to the narratives of baseball games
and detective novels, or the photo of that one perfect

Fourth of July, the lake as still and blue as the sky.
Dear students, you can learn to draw the curtains

closed on difficult things (the drapes are sheer
and often fly apart in dreams). Take a walk,

text your friend, pat the dog. Tomorrow we'll look
at a lovely picture of drifting clouds by Constable.

WHAT I WON'T KNOW

In the garden, I never really care
to cut, unsure as the blade closes
on the slim neck of a fragile stem
I'm not causing some terrible wound.

***

How the two men walking together
on the evening sidewalk know each other.
Why the windows are boarded up.
Why the child keeps looking
over his shoulder. What kind
of everyday tragedy the police car
is speeding toward.

***

Three cruisers surround a rusted car
on the highway, guns drawn on a young
woman, her hands up, her dirty t-shirt
caught in rolls of exposed flesh,
the young man in the passenger seat
holding his head, rocking forward,
why they are there, surrendering.

***

The names of all the plants that grow
inside this garden. It has to be enough
to know they persist in blooming
even after the difficult snow.

TETHER

"You tether an animal, you moor a boat."
—DS Hathaway, *Inspector Lewis*

A boat's moorings
are momentary

its sails will unfurl
like slim feathers.

As animals
we trail our ties

carry with us
ideas of home.

We call out
to migrating birds

to dogs lost
deep in the woods

please come back,
and even those

parted from us
a long time

will find
some little way

to return.

THE EIGHT-BELOW EARTH

I.

After a storm, I walk into the dark garden,
the brush of a pine against my knee

when it should have stood thirty feet
in the moist sky. Everything smelled quietly

of sap and sawdust, the torn trunks
of evergreens. When people who love you

say they would do anything for you,
often they mean it. There are things

you know you yourself could be
brought to do. On the last warm day

I pluck, save, take what I can, before
the yard is covered in snow. Three times,

I'm startled by a gold-coated stranger,
but it's nothing human, just yellow leaves

from the maple tree, pressed by the wind
against the gate.

II.

Snow covers the pine's stump, the delicate
boned maple boughs, embraces the scars

as easily as it enfolds perfection, equalizing
the dead, the wounded, the world that is simply

asleep for the moment. The eight-below
earth suits the way I'm best at love—

not too much to try to hold onto—
one or two bright red birds in a white expanse

of winter snow. When spring comes,
bleeding hearts flower now the pine is gone.

I won't lose too many things if I don't love
too many things. Yet I bury my hands

in black dirt in early June and plant a bed
of annuals, believe once more in the constancy

of marigolds.

IN EARLY EVENING

Everything
around the lake

assents to silence.
All birds

agreed to hush.
All feathers, all fur,

felted thick
with fading light.

The boat comes
to a gentle rest

on the blue cusp
of still water.

Take it with you,
this interlude,

the sweet middle eye
of the storm.

Kirsten Dierking is the author of two previous books of poetry, *Northern Oracle* (Spout Press, 2007) and *One Red Eye* (Holy Cow! Press, 2001). Her poems have been heard on The Writer's Almanac and have appeared in numerous journals and anthologies, including Garrison Keillor's *Good Poems, American Places* and *To Sing Along the Way: Minnesota Women Poets from Pre-Territorial Days to the Present*. She is the recipient of a 2010 McKnight Artist Fellowship, a Minnesota State Arts Board Grant for literature, a Loft Literary Center Career Initiative Grant, a SASE/Jerome Grant, and a writing residency at the Banfill-Locke Center for the Arts. She teaches humanities courses at Anoka-Ramsey Community College. In 2011, Kirsten received the NEA's Excellence in the Academy Award for the Art of Teaching, and in 2009 she received the Building Bridges Award in Education from the Islamic Resource Group of Minnesota.